YOU'RE A CHRISTMAS STAR

YOU'RE A CHRISTMAS STAR

An Hachette UK Company
www.hachette.co.uk

Vie Books, an imprint of Summersdale Publishers Ltd
Part of Octopus Publishing Group Limited
Carmelite House
50 Victoria Embankment
LONDON
EC4Y 0DZ
UK

www.summersdale.com

Printed and bound in China

ISBN: 978-1-83799-173-0

Substantial discounts on bulk quantities of Summersdale books are available to corporations, professional associations and other organizations. For details contact general enquiries: telephone: +44 (0) 1243 771107 or email: enquiries@summersdale.com.

YOU'RE A CHRISTMAS STAR

Fun Activities for a Calm Christmas

Poppy O'Neill

CONTENTS

FOREWORD

Amanda Ashman-Wymbs
Counsellor and Psychotherapist, registered and accredited by
the British Association for Counselling and Psychotherapy

Having raised two girls and working with lots of young people in the private and public sector for many years, it is clear to me that the run-up to Christmas and the festive period can be an unsettling and confusing time for children, both emotionally and psychologically. From excited highs to jealousy, disappointment and deep sadness, its true to say that the Christmas period often brings emotions and psychological states that children can find very hard to manage.

You're a Christmas Star by Poppy O'Neill is a great little supportive exercise book. Aimed at children aged 7–11, it is full of appropriate, fun activities and messages, which will appeal to and engage a child's attention. The book helps and encourages the child to share, identify and understand their feelings, as well as teaching lots of helpful exercises, such as breathing techniques, yoga postures and mindfulness practices, to enable the child to settle and come back to a calm place within. It also supports the child in developing a healthier relationship with themselves and the festive period through awareness of diet and encouraging a connection to the natural world. They are guided on how to process their feelings and practise gratitude, as reflecting on the good in their lives brings a natural joy to the heart.

I highly recommend this book as the content really will help the child to cope with and understand their difficulties, as well as support them in connecting with the love, peace and magic that Christmastime can offer.

INTRODUCTION: A GUIDE FOR PARENTS AND CARERS

You're a Christmas Star is a fun and practical guide to managing feelings during the Christmas period. Using ideas and activities inspired by techniques developed by child psychologists, this book will help your child understand their feelings, providing them with ways to express themselves safely and calmly during the festive season.

Christmas can invoke a plethora of emotions, not least excitement and impatience, which can become overwhelming in the build-up to the big day. It can also bring up more difficult emotions, such as disappointment, jealousy and sadness. There's nothing wrong with any of these emotions, and it's very normal for children to experience a lot of strong feelings at this time of year.

You may be reading this book for a number of reasons: perhaps your child struggles to sleep in the lead-up to Christmas and you're looking for tools to help calm their mind, or maybe you're keen to help them take a less materialistic view of the season. Many children struggle with comparing their Christmas to others' after seeing friends or celebrities celebrating with expensive gifts and lavish decorations. This book will also help if Christmas this year looks different in some way, perhaps because of separation, bereavement or moving house, and you are exploring different ways to make this transition as manageable as possible.

This book is aimed at children aged 7–11, a time when some of the magic of Christmas can start to feel different. Whatever challenges Christmas brings, this book can help your child understand and accept the emotions they experience. If your Christmas isn't perfect, you're certainly not alone. With your support and patience, your child can navigate the highs and lows of the festive season – enjoying and appreciating the magic while finding resilience through the trickier parts. Wishing you a calm, peaceful Christmas!

What to expect during the festive season

Christmas can be a time of great disruption where schedules are full and usual routines are discarded. With everything going on, it's natural for children to experience strong, and often overwhelming, emotions and behave in ways that seem out of character during this time. Here are some of the most common things you might notice about your child:

- Difficulty sleeping

- Short-temperedness

- Increased conflict between siblings

- Focus on the materialistic side of Christmas

- Boredom

- Overtiredness

- Explosive emotions

You'll know best how your child usually responds to the Christmas period, so don't set up expectations that they'll behave perfectly and remain calm throughout – you'll only find yourself getting frustrated and stressed.

It can be difficult to acknowledge that Christmas brings its emotional challenges, as there's so much pressure on parents and carers to make it perfect. Be kind to yourself and let the season unfold in its own unique way, remembering that your relationship with your child is the most special and important part.

How to use this book: For parents and carers

This book is for your child, so the amount of involvement you have will depend on how much they want or need from you. Some children might be happy working through the activities by themselves, while others might need a little guidance and encouragement.

Even if your child prefers to complete the activities alone, it's a good idea to show an interest and start a conversation about the book – anything they've learned or realized, any parts they've found unhelpful or boring. Let this book provide a way to connect and discuss emotions you're both feeling about Christmas, or anything else that's going on in your child's life.

The activities are designed to get your child thinking about their emotions and how they react to them, so reassure them that there are no wrong answers and they can go at their own pace. Hopefully this book will help you and your child gain a greater understanding of each other and help you enjoy the Christmas period. However, if you have any serious concerns about your child's mental health, your doctor is the best person to go to for further advice.

HOW TO USE THIS BOOK:
A GUIDE FOR CHILDREN

Christmas is coming! How does it feel for you? You might be experiencing all sorts of emotions about Christmas, and whatever those feelings may be, it's OK to have them.

This time of year can be difficult to deal with – the waiting, the excitement… and also the parts that might make you feel bored, worried or sad. Here are some things lots of kids find tricky about Christmas:

★ Worrying that something might go wrong

★ Feeling impatient

★ Feeling jealous

★ Struggling to sleep

If that sounds like you, you're not the only one! Lots of children your age struggle with these things, it's just that sometimes they don't show it on the outside. This book is here to help you understand your feelings and enjoy Christmastime.

There are lots of activities and ideas to help you get into the festive spirit, plus ways to help you deal with the tricky bits of Christmas so that you can have a good time with the people close to you. Go at your own pace, there is no rush. If you get stuck at any point, you can get help from your grown-up – this might be a member of your family, carer, a teacher or another adult you know well. This book is for you and about you, so there are no wrong answers – you're the expert!

INTRODUCING
DASH THE CHRISTMAS MONSTER

Hello and merry Christmas! I'm Dash and I'm here to guide you through this book. You'll see me on lots of the pages, having fun alongside you.

I can't wait to show you all the brilliant activities and interesting ideas in this book. Are you ready? Let's go!

PART I: CHRISTMAS IS COMING!

In this part of the book we're going to learn all about you and your Christmas plans and traditions! Everybody's Christmas is unique, so let's begin by finding out about yours.

ACTIVITY: ALL ABOUT ME

First, let's learn all about you! Doodle or write your answers in the tags below. It's OK to leave some blank if you get stuck – you can come back to this page at any time.

My name is...

I am ... years old

My home looks like...

My favourite Christmas food is...

I'm good at...

My best Christmas memory is...

My favourite part of Christmas is...

ACTIVITY: MY HOPES FOR CHRISTMAS

If you had three wishes for this Christmas, what would they be? They can be about gifts you'd like to give or receive, things you'd like to do, foods you'd like to eat or even something magical you wish would happen.

Write or draw your three wishes in the boxes.

ACTIVITY: MY CHRISTMAS TRADITIONS

There are many Christmas traditions – some families follow lots of them, and others just a few. Other people like to do Christmas their own way, or don't celebrate Christmas at all! We're all different.

Christmas traditions include things like decorating a Christmas tree, pulling crackers and putting out a drink and snack for Santa on Christmas Eve. Which traditions do you love to do at Christmastime? They might be the kind lots of people do, like decorating a Christmas tree, or something unique to your family, like a festive film you watch or a place you visit near Christmas.

Draw your traditions in the frames.

ACTIVITY:
I'LL SPEND THIS CHRISTMAS WITH...

Who will you see and spend time with during Christmastime this year? Draw your people and pets here:

Perhaps there's someone who you won't get to see this year at Christmas. Keep them in your heart by drawing them here:

ACTIVITY:
MAKE YOUR OWN COLOURFUL BAUBLES

It feels lovely to give gifts at Christmas, especially those that you've made yourself! Here's a simple craft you can make to give to your loved ones as a present.

You will need:

★ A 12-cm x 16-cm piece of plain or patterned paper

★ Colouring pens or pencils

★ A ruler

★ Scissors

★ 2 split pins

★ Ribbon or string (enough to hang your bauble)

How to:

1. Use your ruler and pencil to divide your paper into eight 2 cm-wide strips. If you're using plain paper, add some colour and patterns. At each end of the strips, draw a dot as a guide for where to put your split pin.

2. Ask a grown-up to help you cut out your strips.

3. Use one split pin to join all eight strips together at one end. You may want to ask an adult to help you with this as it can get a bit tricky.

4. Curl each strip up so the other ends join together in a bauble shape, then fasten those ends together with the other split pin.

5. Tie the ribbon or string around one of the split pins to make a loop, so your bauble can be hung on a Christmas tree.

You can use an empty teabag box or a large, washed yoghurt pot to make sure your handmade baubles don't get squashed. Then wrap them in pretty paper and give them to your friends and loved ones!

CHRISTMASTIME CAN BE TRICKY

There are lots of good things about Christmas – they can be spending time with people we love, putting up twinkly lights, giving and receiving presents, singing Christmas songs… but just like any other time of the year, we can have challenges and difficult feelings at Christmastime. The extra excitement many of us feel at this time of year, plus wanting Christmas to be perfect, can mean we feel even bigger emotions than usual.

It's OK to feel big emotions any time of year. Keep reading to find ways we can be kind to ourselves, find calm and ask for help when we need extra support.

Just because it's Christmas, doesn't mean your emotions need to take time off. You might be feeling:

★ Sad because you're not seeing your school friends

★ Worried that something you don't want will happen in the new year

★ Annoyed with your siblings

… or all sorts of other things! It's OK to feel big emotions.

ALL EMOTIONS
ARE OK

MY GRATITUDE ADVENT CALENDAR

Have you seen those advent calendars with a door to open each morning? Here's another kind of advent calendar, made to help you notice all the brilliant things in the world!

Gratitude is about feeling and showing appreciation for what you are thankful for. Thinking of everything you are grateful for is a great way to remind you of all the wonderful things in life. Gratitude is wonderful for your mind and emotions, because it helps you get into the habit of focusing on the positive, which leads to feeling happier and calmer each day.

In this activity, you'll find a new idea for gratitude each day for 24 days leading up to Christmas. It could be feeling grateful for something big (like a person you love) or small (like a robin singing outside your window).

You can carefully cut out the page (you may need to ask your grown-up for help!) and stick it somewhere in your home where you'll see it every day.

1. A small thing that made you smile today

2. Someone you're thankful for in your life

3. Something you're really good at

4. Something that made you laugh today

5. Something you're proud of

6. Something that went well for you today

7. Something beautiful you noticed today

8. Someone who's helped you recently

9. Something you're looking forward to

10. Something good that happened to you this week

11. A happy Christmas memory you have

12. Something you learned recently

13. A talent or skill you possess that you're grateful for

14. Something that made you feel loved today

15. Something new you tried that you enjoyed

16. Something you're thankful for about your home

17. Something kind someone did for you recently

18. Something in nature that you're grateful for

19. A book, movie or song that you enjoy

20. A favourite possession that you're grateful for

21. Something that helps you feel cosy

22. Something that tasted good recently

23. Something that helps you feel calm

24. Something that makes you feel Christmassy

WHAT DOES CHRISTMAS FEEL LIKE?

We all experience lots of different emotions at Christmastime. We don't feel excitement and happiness all the time!

Dash feels angry that Buddy took the last gingerbread cookie.

Dash takes three deep breaths to calm down, then says, "Bop, I wish you'd made sure everyone got a cookie. They smelled so delicious!"

Can you think of a time you felt angry recently? Draw or write about it here:

Dash's friends are going carol singing. Dash feels anxious about knocking on strangers' doors and singing songs to them.

Dash stands up tall to feel braver, then says, "Will we knock on strangers' doors, or just people we know?"

Dash's friends listen and agree only to knock on the doors of people they know.

Can you think of a time you felt anxious or worried recently? Draw or write about it here:

Dash's cousins live in another country, which means Dash won't get to see them this Christmas. Dash feels sad without them.

Dash starts to cry and finds a grown-up to hug. "I feel sad I won't see them this year," says Dash.

Can you think of a time you felt sad recently? Draw or write about it here:

All feelings are OK, all year round! Christmas is a time to share our true feelings with our loved ones and show each other kindness and understanding.

ACTIVITY: SANTA'S LIST

Imagine Santa wants you and Dash to help him make Christmas special for your loved ones. He gives you both three wishes to choose the dream gifts you'd like to give.

Dash chooses a crown for Rah, a skateboard for Pip and a teddy bear for Jem.

Who would you pick for your three wishes? What gifts would you wish for them? Draw them in the gift boxes below.

TALKING ABOUT FEELINGS

Your family and good friends want to hear what it's like to be you, so don't be afraid to talk to people you trust about how you feel.

Even if you're worried your feelings don't quite make sense, or if you're not sure how they might make the other person feel, your feelings still matter.

When you share your feelings with someone who shows you kindness and understanding, those feelings get a little lighter and easier to carry.

MY FEELINGS
MATTER

PART 2:
HOW TO FEEL CALM WHEN IT'S NEARLY CHRISTMAS

Christmas is coming! Can you feel excitement fizzing around inside you?
There's so much to look forward to, it's so difficult to be patient.
In this part of the book you'll find lots of different ideas that'll help
make this part of Christmastime fun and relaxing.

WHY IT'S HARD TO FEEL CALM WHEN YOU'RE EXCITED

Did you know that the feeling of excitement is very similar to the feeling of anxiety? It's true! Both emotions can feel like this:

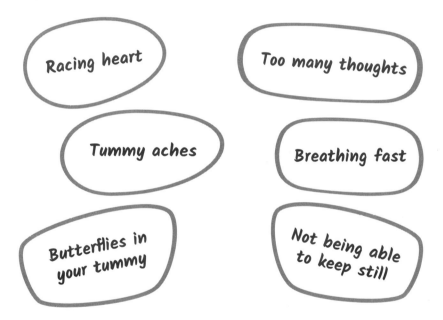

Racing heart

Too many thoughts

Tummy aches

Breathing fast

Butterflies in your tummy

Not being able to keep still

They feel similar partly because they're both feelings we get about the future and the unknown. Our brains feel most relaxed when they know exactly what's going to happen, so having to wait for something in the future is hard! Christmas usually brings lovely surprises such as presents, but sometimes the excitement that we experience can feel similar to anxiety, which can be very confusing.

We can't press a fast-forward button to get to Christmas quicker, so it's a good idea to find ways to calm our emotions while we wait. That way, we can enjoy every day of Christmastime.

ACTIVITY: TAKE A DEEP BREATH

Doing some deep breathing is a quick and simple way to feel calmer. Here are some festive breathing exercises to try.

Snowman breathing

Trace your finger slowly and carefully around the dotted line. Breathe in as your finger moves around the snowman's head, and out as it moves around the snowman's body. The slower you move your finger, the deeper and more even your breaths will become.

Start here

Star breathing

Place your finger on the start button, then slowly and carefully trace your finger around the star, following the instructions written around the edges. Hold your breath for just a moment at each of the points. Move your finger around the star three times or until you feel calm.

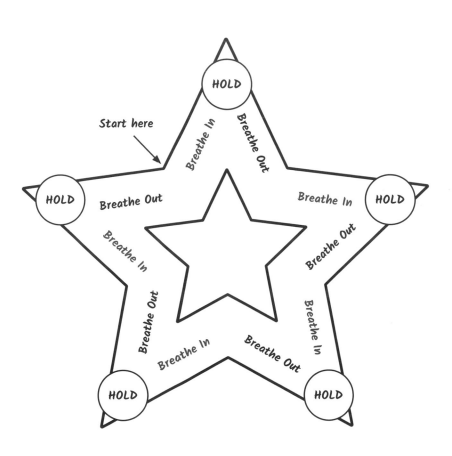

Santa's belly breathing

Imagine you are Santa Claus dressed up cosy and ready to fly around the world! Take some deep breaths to prepare for your big journey.

Place one hand on your belly and take a deep breath in. Can you bring the breath down into your belly, so that it grows big and round, like Santa's? Feel your hand move as your belly gets bigger. As you breathe out, feel your hand move in as your belly gets smaller.

Repeat three times or until you feel ready to stop.

COSY CHRISTMAS YOGA

Yoga is a brilliant way to relax your body and mind. It involves stretching and making shapes with your body, holding them for a few moments, then moving into a new shape. Take it very slowly and if anything hurts or feels uncomfortable, stop and find a comfier position. Let's give it a try.

Christmas tree pose

Stand up straight and put your palms together. Slowly lift your arms above your head so your fingers are pointing towards the ceiling, like a star on top of a Christmas tree. If you feel steady, bring one foot up to your knee and balance. Hold this position for three breaths.

Star pose

Stand with your feet wide apart – as wide as they will comfortably go – and stretch your arms and fingers out wide like a sparkling star! Hold this position for three breaths.

Reindeer pose

Stand up straight with your legs together. Take a step back with one foot – it doesn't have to be a big step, just whatever feels comfortable. Stretch your fingers wide and hold them above your head like mighty antlers. Hold this position for three breaths then swap legs.

Ice skater pose

Stand up straight and find your balance. Standing on your right leg, carefully lift your left leg out behind you. If you are able to, grab your foot with your left hand. Hold your right arm out in front of you to help you balance. Hold this position for three breaths, then switch legs and repeat the steps.

Candy cane pose

Stand up straight and put your hands, palms together, above your head. Gently bend to one side like a candy cane, feeling a lovely stretch along your side. Hold this position for three breaths then swap sides.

Snowy mountain pose

Stand tall with your feet hip-width apart and your arms to your sides, sticking out a little bit. Stretch your hands down and imagine you are a strong, snow-topped mountain. Tilt your face upwards to watch Santa fly through the sky above you. Hold for three breaths.

ACTIVITY: MAKE A SNOWFLAKE

Did you know that no two snowflakes are ever the same? You can make your own unique Christmas snowflakes using just paper and scissors – here's how. Remember to ask a grown-up to help you with the cutting!

You will need:

★ A square piece of paper
(plain, coloured or patterned)

★ Scissors

How to:

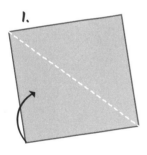

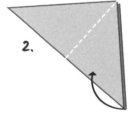

1. Fold your piece of paper in half diagonally.

2. Then fold it in half again.

3. Fold the outer edges into the centre to create a kite shape.

4. Fold your kite in half down the centre.

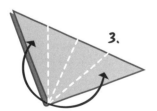

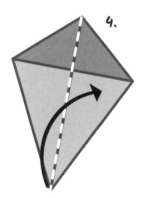

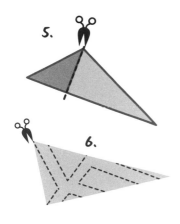

5. Cut off the tip of your kite shape.

6. Use your scissors to snip shapes, lines and patterns into the edges of the triangle. Ask a grown-up to help you and use your imagination, there are no rules!

7. When you're ready, unfold your paper to reveal a unique, beautiful snowflake!

These look lovely stuck to a window with sticky tack!

COPING WITH NEW ROUTINES

A change from our everyday routine can make us feel worried – even exciting changes like having lots of friends and family round that you don't see very often or going somewhere new. Having some calming exercises ready can help you to relax and enjoy these times.

Try this four senses exercise with a friend or a grown-up. Write down or draw your answers in the spaces. It's easy and fun to do.

Find a quiet spot to sit. You could sit on a comfy sofa or a cushion.

Quietly observe and listen to what's going on around you for 1 minute.

When the minute is up, write down:

Three things you can see:

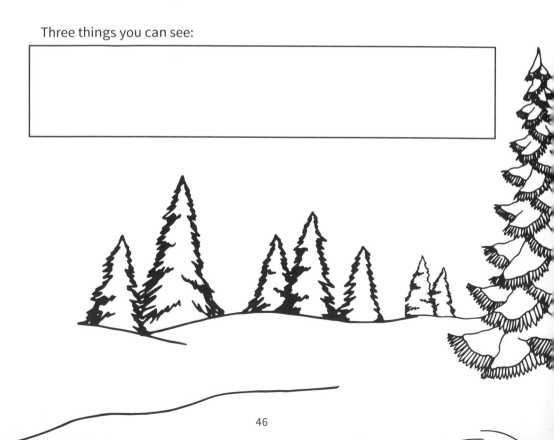

Three things you can hear:

Three things you can touch:

Three things you can smell:

Have you noticed the same things?

THE EMOTION HILL

When a big feeling starts to build inside you – like worry, excitement or anger – it can feel quite scary. Big emotions usually go in the shape of a hill, like this:

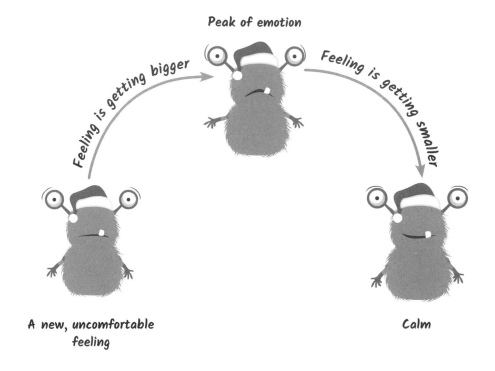

Peak of emotion

Feeling is getting bigger

Feeling is getting smaller

A new, uncomfortable feeling

Calm

If you feel a big emotion starting to go up the hill, imagine this picture: the top of the hill is the peak of the emotion. This can be any emotion – including anxiety, excitement or anger. When you reach this point, it's important to know that your feeling won't last for too long. The emotion might feel quite uncomfortable or difficult. You can take deep breaths and be kind to yourself while you feel it. Soon the emotion will start to go back down the other side, and you will start to feel calmer.

ACTIVITY: SNOWY GLITTER JAR

It feels magical and calming to watch snow fall outside your window at this time of year. But not all of us will get snow at Christmas. Ask a grown-up to help you make a calming glitter jar to recreate a snowy scene indoors!

A glitter jar can help us calm big feelings. Shake up your glitter jar to see the glitter flying everywhere and going bananas! Sometimes our emotions feel like that. Watch as the glitter slowly gets calmer, moves more peacefully and settles on the bottom of the jar. Take deep breaths as you watch and feel your emotions calm like the glitter.

You will need:

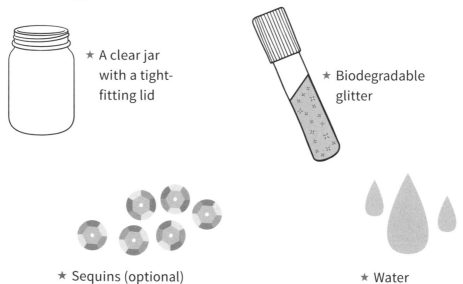

★ A clear jar with a tight-fitting lid

★ Biodegradable glitter

★ Sequins (optional)

★ Water

How to:

1. Ask a grown-up to help you fill your jar with water until it's about half full.

2. Add the glitter and sequins (if you're using them).

3. Carefully top up the jar with water until it's almost full.

4. Replace the lid, making sure it fits firmly. Ask a grown-up to make sure it's on really tight!

5. Shake your glitter jar and watch the glitter come alive!

CALMING MAGIC WORDS

A few calming words can work like magic to help you feel calm when big feelings are bubbling up inside you. Say them out loud, in your head, write them down or colour in the words on this page – you'll find the calming message helps your emotions feel smaller and easier.

Read the statements below and see which ones feel comforting and peaceful to you – everybody's different so some might not feel right for you, and that's OK! When you have finished, colour them in.

My feelings matter

I can try my best

I am strong and capable

I am safe and loved

I can always ask for help

I am surrounded by people who care about me

I am calm
and
peaceful

I can take deep
breaths

I am kind to myself
and others

I am
brave and
courageous

I can
make good
choices

I am grateful
for all the
good things
in my life

Waiting
is hard,
and I can
do hard
things

ACTIVITY: HELP DASH TO FEEL CALM

The weather forecast says it will snow where Dash lives tomorrow. Dash loves to build snowmen and is making plans to have a snowball fight with Fizz and Pip. Dash feels so excited that it might snow, and at the same time, worried that the weather forecast could be wrong.

Dash is finding it very difficult to relax!

Can you think of three tips to help Dash feel calmer? Write or draw them in the boxes.

What can you spot in the picture that might help Dash?

Answer: Play with the snowy glitter jar, do some yoga, make some paper snowflakes or look at the gratitude calendar.

I CAN ASK
FOR HELP

MINDFUL MOMENTS

Practising mindfulness often means focusing all your attention on what is happening right now. It's a wonderful way to help yourself enjoy every moment of the festive season.

You can take a mindful moment any time, anywhere! Practising mindfulness regularly is really good for you! Here are some ideas to try:

Slow down and appreciate the taste, smell and texture of a meal or snack you eat.	How do your clothes feel? Touch the fabric and feel its texture against your skin.	Pick a Christmas decoration and take time to look at it closely – notice every detail.
Can you find something in your home that smells good? Take a moment to enjoy its scent.	Listen to the sounds of nature outside your window.	Place your hand on your heart and feel your heart beating.
Take some deep breaths and feel the air moving in and out of your nostrils.	Listen to a Christmas song and pay attention to the feel of your body as you move to the music.	Sing a Christmas carol and feel the sensation of your voice in your throat.

Mindfulness golden rules

★ Slow down

★ Pay attention to your senses

★ Look for the beauty in every moment

PART 3:
TAKING GOOD CARE OF
YOURSELF OVER CHRISTMAS

Looking after your body and mind is important all year round! It can be tricky at Christmas because our routines are different and there are different foods to enjoy. In this part of the book you'll find lots of ideas for staying healthy and well during Christmastime.

ACTIVITY: EATING A CHRISTMAS RAINBOW

It's lovely to have special Christmassy food at this time of year. Combine sweets and treats with a healthy balanced diet to keep your body and mind feeling good.

Colour in the Christmas rainbow of food – which ones will you eat this year?

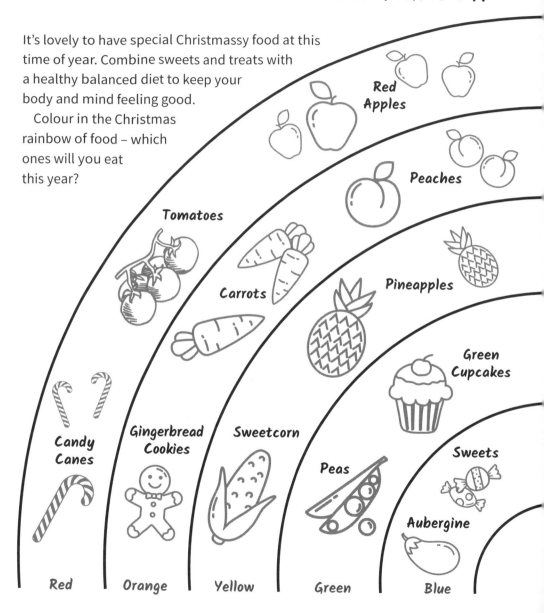

Red Apples

Peaches

Tomatoes

Carrots

Pineapples

Green Cupcakes

Candy Canes

Gingerbread Cookies

Sweetcorn

Peas

Sweets

Aubergine

Red   Orange   Yellow   Green   Blue

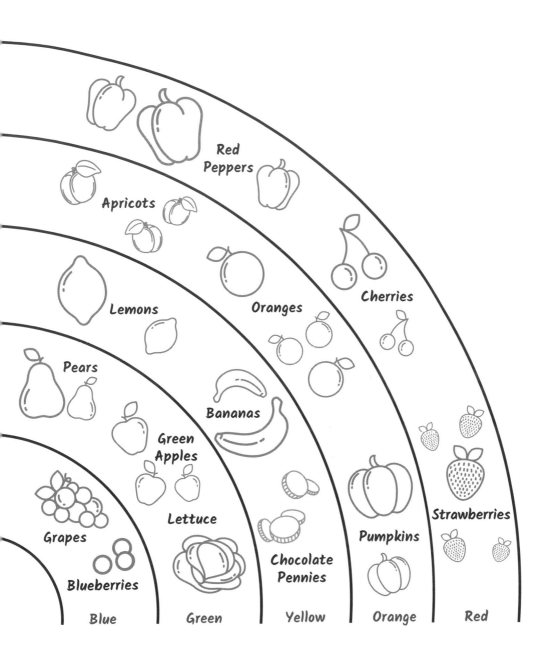

Red Peppers

Apricots

Lemons

Oranges

Cherries

Pears

Bananas

Green Apples

Strawberries

Grapes

Lettuce

Pumpkins

Blueberries

Chocolate Pennies

Blue

Green

Yellow

Orange

Red

KEEPING WARM

In the northern hemisphere, Christmas comes at the coldest time of year. For those in the southern hemisphere, Christmas happens during the summer!

While it's cold, keeping our bodies warm is an important part of taking care of ourselves each day. When we feel warm and cosy, we can relax and enjoy ourselves more.

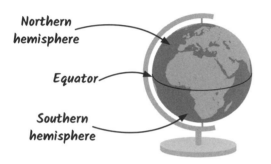

Northern hemisphere

Equator

Southern hemisphere

Northern hemisphere: the part of the world north of the equator. Southern hemisphere: the part of the world south of the equator.

Ways to keep warm in cold weather:

★ Wear lots of layers of clothing: warm air gets trapped between the layers, helping you stay cosy.

★ Drink something warm: add some hot water to a drink of juice, or warm up milk on the stove (ask a grown-up to help you!).

★ Cuddle up close: sharing our bodies' heat with loved ones and pets is a comforting way to warm up quickly.

★ Move your body: when you move around – walking, dancing, jumping, running, climbing – your heartrate increases, which makes your whole body warm up.

ACTIVITY: DRESS UP WARM!

Help Dash pick out warm clothes for a snowy day. Draw a circle around the clothes you think Dash should wear out in the cold.

GETTING OUTDOORS WHEN IT'S COLD

Staying cosy inside feels really good when it's cold outside. But getting outside for at least a little while each day will help keep your mind and body healthy and feeling good.

Here are some fun outdoor activities to try.

Outdoor treasure hunt

Hide small objects along your walk or in your garden, then get your family to find them! You could hide:

★ Christmas baubles
★ Chocolate coins
★ Small toys

★ Messages or clues written on paper
★ Carrots or other vegetables
★ Painted stones

Snowball target practice

If it snows where you live, draw a target on a wall with chalk, or in the snow with a stick, and practise throwing snowballs to hit the bullseye.

Nature's art supplies

You don't need to go to the shop to find Christmassy art supplies – you can find them outdoors! Look around your garden or on your next walk for things like…

★ Pinecones to paint

★ Ivy for a wreath

★ Fallen leaves to take a rubbing of

★ Sticks to transform into magic wands

★ Feathers for a collage

Remember to always check with your grown-up what you can any can't touch while you are out and about!

Next time you're in nature, keep an eye out for anything you could use for your art. Write or draw your findings in the space below.

Winter sketching

Take this book (or a notebook) and pencils on a walk and stop to draw any details or views you find interesting and inspiring. Look closely and you'll find something beautiful in every hedgerow, path or tree! Draw what you find here:

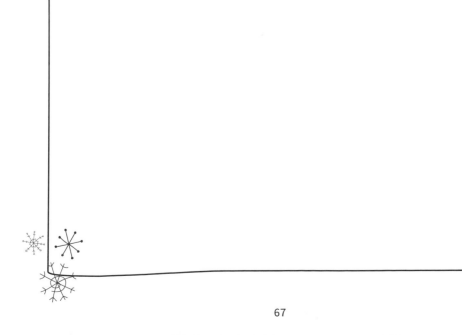

ACTIVITY: MAKE MULLED APPLE JUICE

Adding spices to drinks and warming them up is a traditional way to keep warm during the colder months – it also tastes delicious! This is called "mulling" and people have been doing it for hundreds of years.

You will need:

★ 1 litre apple juice

★ 1 orange, washed

★ 10 cloves

★ 1 cinnamon stick (optional)

★ 1 tsp honey

How to:

1. Pour the apple juice into a saucepan and ask a grown-up to help you turn the hob on at a low heat.

2. Use a vegetable peeler to peel thin strips off a washed orange – just the outer part that is very orange. Don't worry if you get some white bits too. You can eat the orange as a snack while you wait for your mulled apple juice!

3. Put the cloves and cinnamon stick into the pan with your warm apple juice. These will make your mulled apple juice smell and taste amazing.

4. Add the honey to the apple juice mixture.

5. Let your apple juice warm gently for about 15 minutes – keep it on a low heat so it doesn't boil.

6. Ask an adult to take the mulled apple juice off the heat and use a slotted spoon or sieve to scoop the cinnamon, cloves and orange peel out – they leave their wonderful flavours in the juice, but they don't taste good to eat!

7. Pour the mulled apple juice into mugs and once it's cooled down a little, it's ready to drink!

THE WINTER SOLSTICE

In the northern hemisphere, the winter solstice happens just a few days before Christmas Day, on the 20, 21 or 22 of December each year. This day is the shortest day of the year. There are still 24 hours like every other day but it is the day the sun is in the sky for the shortest time. The sun rises late and sets early – have you noticed how it's dark when you wake up in the winter?

After the winter solstice, the sun sets a little later each day, until the summer solstice in June, which is the longest day of the year, which has the longest time between sunrise and sunset.

> In the southern hemisphere, it's the opposite – the longest day of sunlight is in December, and the shortest is in June.

Sunlight is important for our bodies and minds to stay healthy, for many reasons:

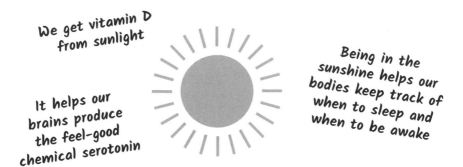

We get vitamin D from sunlight

It helps our brains produce the feel-good chemical serotonin

Being in the sunshine helps our bodies keep track of when to sleep and when to be awake

During the winter there isn't as much sunlight, so it's important to get outdoors during the day, even if it's not very sunny or warm!

Solstice facts:

* Go outside at noon on the winter solstice. If it's not cloudy, look at your shadow; it will be the longest one you have all year!

* The solstice is celebrated in different ways all over the world. Some celebrate by lighting bonfires and candles, and eating special foods.

* The solstice marks the first day of winter in the astronomical calendar.

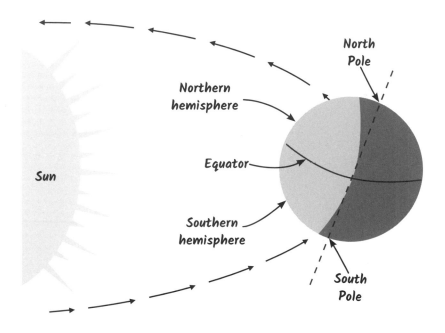

The earth is tilted – when the northern hemisphere is tilted away from the sun it's winter there. At the same time the southern hemisphere is tilted towards it, so it's summer there!

ACTIVITY: DESIGN A COSY CHILL-OUT ZONE

Chilling out and feeling relaxed is a really important part of taking care of our bodies and minds. When we feel cosy, comfy and calm, our bodies and minds can recharge and we can get creative and express our feelings and emotions.

Can you design a chill-out zone in a cosy corner?

Here are some ideas…

★ Squishy cushions

★ Interesting books

★ Soft blankets

★ A cuddly toy

★ A warm drink

★ Calm music

★ Snuggly slippers or socks

★ Twinkly lights

★ A cosy jumper

Draw your chill-out zone:

ACTIVITY: WONDERFUL WATER

Water is essential for every part of our bodies, because our bodies are made up of about 60 per cent water. We need water to make sure our bodies stay the right temperature, as well as to keep our blood flowing and brain cells growing. When we haven't had enough to drink, our emotions can feel bigger and we might feel angry more quickly too.

Imagine a plant – when you give it a drink of water, its leaves get shinier and stronger, its stalk grows and it might even produce flowers!

Colour in the plants so you can tell they've had plenty to drink and are super healthy!

Scientists and doctors recommend kids your age need to drink about 1.5 litres of water per day to support your growing body. This is about 6–8 cups of water or other healthy drinks like milk, plant-based milk, juice or squash.

Cool water facts:

Reindeer are brilliant swimmers.

Snowflakes are made of frozen water and they all have six sides or arms.

It's quite difficult to get drinking water in the Arctic, where Santa lives. It can't be made by melting the ice there, because it is made from salt water. Drinking water can be made from melting snow, which is made of rainwater.

Ice skating was invented in Scandinavia around 1000 BCE, and the first skates were made of elk, oxen and reindeer bones.

If you have a natural Christmas tree, it needs a drink of water every day.

WRAP UP WARM!

GET CREATIVE!

Creativity is when you use your imagination to think up or make something new. Creativity is wonderful for our minds because when we create something – like a drawing, game or outfit – it allows us to express and share our ideas and emotions. Creating something unique can help you feel happy and proud. What's more, when you are being creative, you focus on what you are creating, rather than on your worries.

There are so many ways to be creative! Here are just a few:

Drawing

Dancing

Singing

Playing an instrument

Writing a story or poem

Making up a play

Inventing a game

Painting

Coding

Playing with toys

Making a collection

Baking

Crafting

Dressing up

Playing make believe

Draw a circle around the creative activities you love best (or ones you'd like to try!) – add your own ideas if you don't see your favourites here.

ACTIVITY: CHRISTMAS DOODLES

Can you add creative details to this Christmassy picture? Decorate the trees, add people, animals, gifts, food, inventions… whatever you love to create the most.

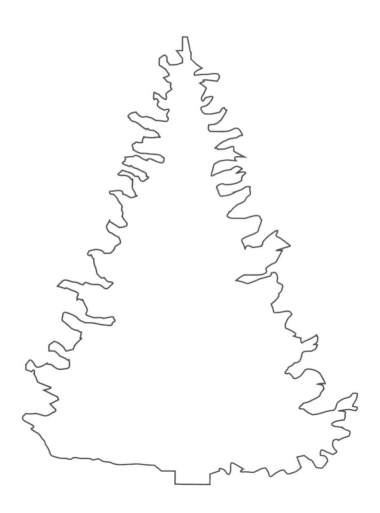

COSY INDOOR CHALLENGE

How many of the cosy indoor activities on this list can you try this Christmas? Tick them off as you go!

Watch a Christmas movie with your loved ones ☐

Make a homemade Christmas card ☐

Decorate cookies or gingerbread cookies ☐

Write a Christmas poem and share it with your family ☐

Read a Christmas story ☐

Write a letter to Santa ☐

Make a paper snowflake for your window (see page 44) ☐

Act out a Christmas story ☐

Learn a Christmas carol by heart ☐

Keep a Christmas journal ☐

Have a game night ☐

Make a scavenger hunt for your family ☐

SPREAD KINDNESS AT CHRISTMAS

PART 4:
I CAN'T SLEEP!

Going to sleep can be extra tricky around Christmas – as excitement builds for Christmas Day, it gets difficult to switch off and relax at bedtime. In this part of the book we'll explore why this is and find out about lots of ideas to help you to feel calm so you are able to get plenty of sleep.

WHY IS GOING TO SLEEP SO DIFFICULT?

We all know that the sooner we fall asleep, the sooner it'll be Christmas Day. So why does it get trickier and trickier to fall asleep at this time of year?

The answer is emotions! Just like we learned in Part 2, how we feel when we are excited is very similar to what happens in our bodies when we feel anxious, because it makes our bodies feel fizzy and our minds race quickly from thought to thought. We might also be dealing with other emotions such as sadness, anger or disappointment – these don't stop just because it's Christmas.

It can feel like an adventure to stay up late at Christmastime, but if we're not getting enough sleep it can make us grumpy and upset in the day time. So, if you're finding it difficult to fall asleep at night, it's a great idea to find ways to help yourself relax. Not all the ideas in this part of the book will work for everybody – give them all a try, pick the ones that help you and leave the rest!

ACTIVITY: BEDTIME ROUTINES

Everybody's bedtime routine is different! Dash's bedtime routine goes like this:

★ Take a bath and brush my teeth

★ Put on my pyjamas

★ Share a story with my grown-ups

★ Talk about my day and my feelings

★ Cuddles goodnight

★ Time for sleeping

On the night before Christmas, Dash does some extra things at bedtime:

★ Make a snack for Santa and his reindeer

★ Take a bath and brush my teeth

★ Put on pyjamas

★ Lay out my stocking

★ Share a story with my grown-ups

★ Talk about my day and my feelings

★ Cuddles goodnight

★ Time for sleeping

Dash finds it quite difficult to go to sleep when there are changes to the bedtime routine. That's why Dash keeps all the regular parts of bedtime, even on a special night!

What's your regular bedtime routine? Write or draw about it here:

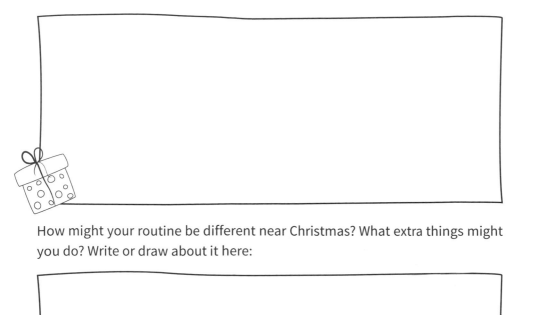

How might your routine be different near Christmas? What extra things might you do? Write or draw about it here:

If you're adding extra exciting things to your bedtime routine, you might also like to add some extra calming things too. These will help you relax your body and mind, ready for sleep. Keep reading to find some great ideas.

ACTIVITY: GUIDED SNOWFLAKE MEDITATION

Visualization is a way of relaxing your body and your mind at the same time. Read this meditation to yourself and then imagine it, or ask a grown-up to read it to you. This is a wonderful meditation to help you drift off to sleep. Try it at bedtime!

Get cosy in your bed and close your eyes. Notice how you are feeling. Perhaps you're feeling excited, anxious, sad… all feelings are OK. You can just notice that they are there. You can enjoy Christmas one moment at a time by relaxing. Let's enjoy this moment by imagining soft snow falling under the light of the moon. Concentrate on one single snowflake, as it falls very, very slowly from a fluffy cloud. Using your mind, can you slow down the snowflake's fall even more? Let your snowflake fall in slow motion so you can see its beautiful patterns as it drifts, ever so slowly through the air. See your snowflake dance very slowly with the other snowflakes around it.

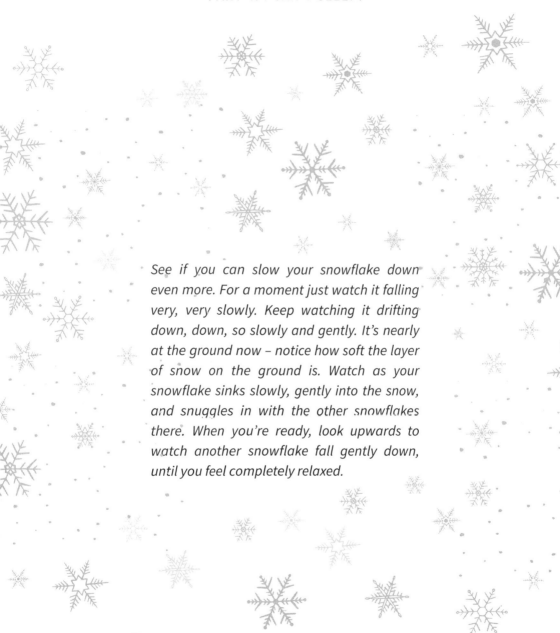

See if you can slow your snowflake down even more. For a moment just watch it falling very, very slowly. Keep watching it drifting down, down, so slowly and gently. It's nearly at the ground now – notice how soft the layer of snow on the ground is. Watch as your snowflake sinks slowly, gently into the snow, and snuggles in with the other snowflakes there. When you're ready, look upwards to watch another snowflake fall gently down, until you feel completely relaxed.

ACTIVITY: CALMING BODY SCAN

If your body feels fizzy and full of energy when it's time to sleep, try this body wriggle and scan!
Here's how:

1. Get comfy in bed.

2. Notice your fizzy feelings and let your body wriggle about, showing your feelings.

3. When you're ready, let your body be still and close your eyes.

4. Start at the top of your body. Focus your attention on the top of your head and then work your way down to your forehead and then your eyes. Notice each body part as you scan past it. As you go past your mouth and nose, notice your breathing. What sensations are you aware of?

5. Keep your attention moving slowly down your body like a laser beam. Can you feel the fabric of your pyjamas?

6. As your attention moves slowly down your body, become aware of what you can feel. Is there any tightness or tingling? Any feelings are OK, just notice any sensations you feel in your body.

7. If your mind wanders, that's OK. Just bring your attention back to the body part that you got to.

8. Keep going until you reach the tips of your toes.

DREAMING OF CHRISTMAS

ACTIVITY: CALM COLOURING

Before you start your bedtime routine, you might like to try a calming evening activity like colouring. The earlier you begin relaxing, the easier it will be to get to sleep.

Colour in this calm Christmas picture.

Scientists believe that the most calming colours to look at and colour with are blue, turquoise, light pink and purple. They also found that lighter colours are more calming than darker ones.

A SLEEPY CHRISTMAS TALE

Read this story at bedtime to help you get to sleep. Reading books helps you feel sleepy because it helps your mind relax.

One Christmas Eve, Dash loaded up a sack with gifts for special friends. There was a gift for Frog, a gift for Hedgehog and a gift for Bear.

Dash was feeling full of excitement for Christmas Day!

First, Dash arrived at Frog's home. Dash knocked on the door, eager to give Frog her Christmas gift. But there was no answer. Dash felt disappointed.

"I'll knock one more time," thought Dash, "then I'll go to Hedgehog's house." Dash knocked one more time, but there was no answer.

Dash walked sadly away from Frog's house. "I'll give Frog her gift after Christmas," thought Dash. "That'll make Christmas last a little bit longer!"

At this thought, Dash felt excited again.

Soon, Dash reached Hedgehog's home and knocked at the door.

Dash waited a moment, then knocked again.

But there was no answer.

"Oh no," thought Dash, "have all of my friends gone away for Christmas? Are they at a party together, without me?"

Bear lived next door to Hedgehog, and Dash looked sadly at Bear's door. Dash wasn't sure whether to knock or to just go home. But then, Dash heard a sound coming from inside Bear's house.

Dash pressed one ear up to Bear's door. A big grin spread across Dash's face. "Snoring!" Dash exclaimed.

Dash peeked through Bear's window and sure enough, there was Bear, sleeping peacefully.

Dash was just about to creep quietly away when Bear stirred, opened one eye and locked eyes with Dash.

Bear grinned back, yawned, stretched and opened his front door.

Dash was so pleased to see Bear.

"I got you a present," said Dash. "Why were you sleeping? It's the middle of the day!"

Bear yawned happily and accepted Dash's gift. "I'm sleeping because it's what bears do in the winter."

Dash felt confused. "Why?"

"When it's cold and there isn't much food around, it makes sense to have a big meal and get cosy until the spring," Bear said. "Lots of animals in this neighbourhood do it. Our friends Frog and Hedgehog, for example."

Dash felt so relieved. "That's why they didn't come to their doors!"

"That's right," said Bear. "Shall we open our presents? I got you something too."

The two friends exchanged gifts and laughed – they'd both chosen a soft blanket to give each other.

"Maybe I'll have a little snooze too," said Dash.

The end

I FEEL CALM
AND READY
FOR SLEEP

ACTIVITY: SLEEPY CHRISTMAS EVE DRINK

Try this calming warm drink before bed on Christmas Eve. You could even make it part of your Christmas traditions!

You will need:

★ 1 cup of cow, almond or oat milk

★ 1 tsp honey

★ ½ tsp vanilla extract

★ A sprinkle of ground cinnamon

Cow, oat and almond milk all contain a chemical called tryptophan, which helps you fall asleep.

How to:

1. Pour milk into a pan and ask a grown-up to help you warm it up on a low heat.

2. Add the honey and vanilla to the milk and stir.

3. When the milk is warmed, pour it into your favourite mug and sprinkle cinnamon on top.

4. Once it's cooled down enough to sip, drink and enjoy!

ACTIVITY: BED SNOW ANGEL STRETCHES

Stretching can help to release tension and emotions from your body after a busy day and get you ready for sleeping.

First lie down on your bed – lying on top of the bed covers is best as it leaves you more room to stretch.

Stretch out your arms and legs and move them from side to side – see how big you can make your bed covers snow angel!

Angels are traditionally found at the top of the Christmas tree. Can you decorate this angel?

ACTIVITY: MY BEDROOM

What does your bedroom look like? Draw it here:

Where we sleep makes a difference to how well we sleep! Take time to make sure your bedroom is comfy and tidy, as this will help you feel relaxed.

WHAT TO DO IF YOU REALLY CAN'T SLEEP

Sometimes, no matter what you try, you just can't get to sleep. Worrying that you won't get to sleep can make it even more difficult to fall asleep! Next time you're struggling to get to sleep, take a moment to think. Do you need:

★ To share a worry with a grown-up?

★ A cuddle?

★ To stretch or get more comfy?

★ A sip of water?

★ To use the toilet?

★ An extra blanket?

If you've made sure you don't need any of these things and you still can't get to sleep, it's OK. You can let go of worrying about getting to sleep. Just resting your eyes and lying quiet and cosy is enough. Think about a lovely dream you'd like to have, taking time to imagine all the details. Rest and relax as much as you can, and you'll be OK.

If you don't get to sleep, you'll probably feel tired tomorrow, but that's not the end of the world. In the morning, let your grown-up know that you couldn't get to sleep and that you're feeling tired. This will help them understand how you're feeling and give them a better idea of how they can help you throughout the day.

I CAN LET GO OF WORRIES

PART 5:
IT'S CHRISTMAS DAY!

Let's celebrate! In this part of the book you'll find ideas and activities to try throughout the day. Don't worry if you don't get through it all today, as you can pick it up again when you're ready. Happy Christmas!

ACTIVITY: CHRISTMAS DAY JOURNALLING

Whatever time of day it is, take a moment to notice how you're feeling – here are some questions to get you writing (or drawing!).

Did you have any dreams in the night? What do you remember of them?

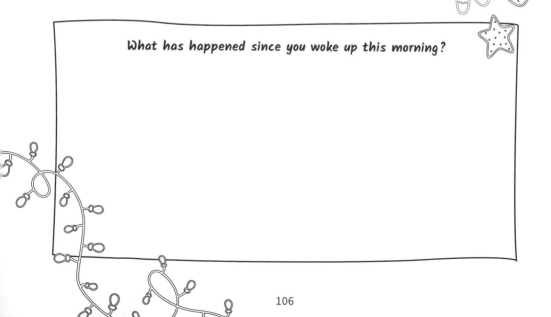

What has happened since you woke up this morning?

What is a Christmas memory you love to think about?

What emotions are you feeling at the moment?

What are your hopes for the rest of the day?

Journalling means writing about what you are thinking and how you are feeling. It's a great way to explore ideas, express emotions and get to know yourself!

ACTIVITY: ENJOY EVERY MOMENT

Dash loves opening gifts and playing with new toys, but there's magic to be found in every moment! Can you write or draw something you're grateful for, a special moment or a happy thought in each of the baubles?

COPING WITH BUSY TIMES

Sometimes Christmas gets busy and loud and it can feel overwhelming. If you feel like this, you're not alone!

When you need to take a break from the hustle and bustle of Christmas, there are a number of things you can do:

COPING WITH QUIET TIMES

It's also true that some parts of Christmas can feel boring or slow – and that's difficult too! We often think Christmas is going to be non-stop fun, so it can feel disappointing when there's a quiet moment.

When Dash feels bored at Christmas…

ACTIVITY: MY GRATITUDE LIST

Dash is writing a gratitude list, thinking about all the things that are wonderful about Christmas Day.

I'm grateful for...

★ **A yummy breakfast**

★ **My cosy home**

★ **New fluffy socks**

★ **Spending the day with my favourite monsters**

★ **A robin landing outside my bedroom window**

★ **The game I really wanted**

★ **Chocolate coins**

What's on your gratitude list? Think about the things you feel thankful for, or lucky to have today.

★

★

★

★

★

★

★

ACTIVITY: WHAT'S SANTA UP TO TODAY?

Have you ever heard the phrase "put yourself in their shoes"? It means imagining you're somebody else and thinking about how they might be feeling. This kind of imagining is called empathy.

When we use empathy, it helps us to understand those around us, reminds us that we are all different and that everybody has feelings that matter.

Can you imagine you're in Santa's shoes on Christmas Day? What might Santa be doing, and how might he be feeling?

Write or draw your ideas.

What will he have for breakfast?

What time did he finish delivering presents?

What emotions is he experiencing?   How might he care for his body today?

How might he care for his mind today?

ACTIVITY: CHRISTMAS COLOURING

Colour in the Christmas picture.
How many helpers can you spot?

Answer: 18 helpers

I AM
BRILLIANT
EXACTLY
AS I AM

ACTIVITY: WHAT'S ON THE MENU?

Christmas is a time when we can share special food together. What's on the menu for you and your loved ones today?

Breakfast

Snacks

Drinks

Treats

Main Course

Sides

Dessert

ACTIVITY: MAKE A CHRISTMAS ALPHABET

Here's a game you can play by yourself or with others. The rules are simple: just think of something Christmas-related for every letter of the alphabet. A couple have been done for you! If you're playing with others, the first person to get to Z is the winner!

A *Advent*

B

C

D

E

F

G

H *Holly*

I

J

K

L _____

M _____

N _____

O _____

P _____

Q _____

R *Reindeer* _____

S _____

T _____

U _____

V _____

W _____

X _____

Y _____

Z _____

ACTIVITY: TIME TO CHILL OUT

Take a break and do some calming Christmas colouring!
How many rabbits can you see?

Answer: There are three rabbits

ACTIVITY: CHRISTMAS SURPRISES

Christmas can be full of surprises and wonderful things you feel grateful for. But sometimes, if you have expected a particular gift, feeling or experience that you didn't get, it can lead to you feeling disappointed.

Try not to have any expectations and instead embrace not knowing what you are going to get or what you might do. This can make Christmas even more exciting and help you to not feel disappointed!

Can you think of any surprises that you have experienced at Christmastime that have been really fun and unexpected? Write or draw about them in the box.

PART 6:
AFTER CHRISTMAS

Christmas Day is over but there's still lots of the Christmas season left.
This can be a much quieter time after an exciting and busy few days!
In this part of the book you'll find ideas and activities for
the time between Christmas Day and New Year's Day.

ENJOYING TWIXTMAS

Some people call the time between Christmas Day and New Year's Day "Twixtmas".

Perhaps your family have lots of things planned for this week, such as visiting friends or going to special places. Maybe it'll be a quiet time for chilling out, or a mix of both.

Here are some fun ideas for activities to do in Twixtmas week.

Make a collage with leftover wrapping paper

Sort through old toys and books – see if there are any you could give to charity

Create a scrap book of memories from this year

Build a den using blankets

Play a board game

Watch a Christmas movie

Draw or paint a self-portrait

Write thank-you notes for your gifts

Learn to code

Make up a play and perform it for your family

Write a story

Design and make a new board game

ACTIVITY: TWIXTMAS CALENDAR

Fill in the calendar with something for each day – you can choose from the stars on the previous page or come up with your own ideas!

26 Boxing Day	27	28
29	30	31 New Year's Eve

1 New Year's Day

ACTIVITY:
MY END-OF-YEAR REFLECTIONS

Think about the year that's coming to an end. What's it been like for you? Let's take some time to reflect. Write or draw your ideas below.

This year on my birthday I turned ... years old

I felt happy when...

I felt annoyed when...

I feel grateful for...

My wish for next Christmas is...

My highlight of the year...

Someone new I met this year...

Something new I tried this year...

I was a good friend when I...

ACTIVITY: A BRAND NEW YEAR

Soon, it'll be a new year! Complete the new year here and colour in the picture.

ACTIVITY: LOOKING AHEAD

Look ahead to the new year through these magic glasses… what can you see?

One goal for next year...

I'm looking forward to...

STORIES OF CHRISTMAS

Every home and family is unique, and that means every Christmas is unique! Here are some kids' stories of their own Christmases.

> **I like going to school and having a routine, so Christmastime can feel difficult for me, even though I want to join in with the fun. My family helped me make a new routine over Christmas so that made it easier for me to feel calm and enjoy it. I love opening the door each morning on my advent calendar – and chocolate too!**
>
> Lucas, 9

> **My parents aren't together so we have two Christmases each year – one at Mum's and one at Dad's. It's cool to get two special days and two sets of presents, but it can be exhausting too! It felt pretty strange at first but now it feels normal. I sometimes wish there were more Christmas movies about families like mine.**
>
> Amelia, 11

> **We don't celebrate Christmas because my family is Muslim, so it feels weird when all the shops are full of Christmas things, my friends are all talking about it and school closes! We use the time off to visit family and do other fun things. We celebrate Eid at a different time of year, with presents and yummy food.**
>
> Omar, 7

THE END

You've reached the end of the book! Dash has had a brilliant Christmas with you! You can come back to this book next Christmas, or any time you feel like you need a boost during a special time. You've done so well and you should be very proud of yourself.

Don't forget: you are unique and your feelings matter, every day of the year!

For parents and carers: Helping your child cope with Christmas

We all want our kids to have a perfect Christmas, but it never quite turns out that way! Changes to the routine, excitement and busy days all add up to big feelings for everyone – including parents. So, it's important to keep in mind at this time of year that perfection is not what your child needs from you. You doing your best and making time to care for yourself as well as connect with your child over the Christmas period is what they need the most.

If Christmas gets overwhelming for you – there's always so much to do, after all – it's worth taking stock of what's important and considering doing less or doing things differently. The Christmas you give your child needs space in it for you to enjoy yourself as well, so remember to leave room for self-care.

Your child may find themselves comparing your Christmas to other families' – looking at the decorations, plans and gifts their friends are expecting and feeling bad about themselves. Try to focus your and your child's attention on the things money can't buy – connection and quality time together. It's hard when kids feel like the odd one out, but when it comes down to it, they appreciate what really matters – even if they don't always show it outwardly.

There will be inevitable ups and downs at Christmas – just like any other time of year – because your and your child's emotions don't take days off. But the added pressure of Christmas can make big feelings seem like more of a problem than they are. So, if your child is grumpy, sad or worried when you think they should be happy, don't sweat it. Letting your child's emotions be what they are will help them to feel calm and more relaxed during what can be a stressful time for everybody.

Showing your child that they are loved and accepted, however they are feeling, will help grow their resilience, self-esteem and empathy. As your child grows, they will be secure in the knowledge that you are on their team no matter what.

I hope this book has been helpful for you and your child. Christmas can be a difficult time to navigate, and you're doing a great job by acknowledging their feelings and guiding them through the highs and lows of the season.

Wishing you a calm Christmas and a peaceful new year!

Further advice

If you're worried about your child's mental health, talk it through with your doctor. While almost all children experience emotional ups and downs at Christmastime, some may benefit from extra support. There are lots of great resources out there for information and guidance on children's mental health. Here are just a few:

YoungMinds Parents' Helpline (UK)
www.youngminds.org.uk
0808 802 5544

BBC Bitesize (UK)
www.bbc.co.uk/bitesize/support

Childline (UK)
www.childline.org.uk
0800 1111

Child Mind Institute (USA)
www.childmind.org

The Youth Mental Health Project (USA)
www.ymhproject.org

Recommended reading

For children:
The Dog That Saved Christmas by Nicola Davies
Barrington Stoke, 2018

My Feelings and Me by Poppy O'Neill
Vie, 2022

Wreck This Journal by Keri Smith
Penguin, 2013

For adults:
It's OK Not to Share, and Other Renegade Rules for Raising Competent and Compassionate Kids by Heather Shumaker
TarcherPerigee, 2012

Good Inside: A Practical Guide to Becoming the Parent You Want to Be by Dr Becky Kennedy
HarperCollins Publishers, 2022

The Story Cure: An A–Z of Books to Keep Kids Happy, Healthy and Wise by Ella Berthoud and Susan Elderkin
Canongate, 2016

Credits

Other books in the series...

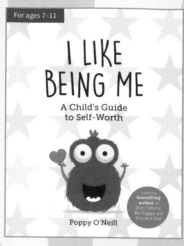

Paperback
ISBN: 978-1-80007-689-1

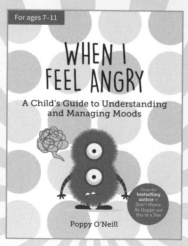

Paperback
ISBN: 978-1-80007-690-7

Other Vie books for parents, carers and children...

Paperback
ISBN: 978-1-80007-721-8

Paperback
ISBN: 978-1-80007-720-1

Paperback
ISBN: 978-1-80007-337-1

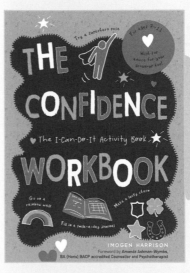

Paperback
ISBN: 978-1-80007-168-1

Have you enjoyed this book?
If so, why not write a review on your favourite website?

If you're interested in finding out more about our books,
find us on Facebook at **Summersdale Publishers**,
on Twitter at **@Summersdale** and on Instagram
and TikTok at **@summersdalebooks** and get in touch.
We'd love to hear from you!

Thanks very much for buying this Summersdale book.

www.summersdale.com